The Online Dating Bible:
33 Proven Commandments to Create a Stunning Profile, Write Alluring Messages, and Get All the Dates You Can Handle

By Patrick King

Dating and Social Skills Coach at www.PatrickKingConsulting.com

The Online Dating Bible: 33 Proven Commandments to Create a Stunning Profile, Write Alluring Messages, and Get All the Dates You Can Handle

Introduction

1. You're online dating? Own it.

2. Online dating is the new organic.

3. Free sites are fine.

4. Seeing people you know is just like running into them at a bar.

5. Curate your online presence

6. Online dating for women is not online dating for men.

7. Don't rely only on online dating.

8. Don't discount sites that are "only for hookups".

9. Profiles actually matter.

10. Scope out your competition.

11. Don't answer profile questions literally.

12. Don't talk about things that can be easily disproved.

13. But do editorialize in your profile.

14. Invest in your pictures.

15. Brag with caution.

16. Perform constant eye-roll checks.

17. Spellchck your profile and messages.

18. Humor usually needs congruent body language.

19. Stories are king; adjective lists are not.

20. You won't appeal to everyone.

21. Re-think what you want in a partner.

22. Don't be paranoid, but be smart.

23. Don't assume exclusivity.

24. Messaging and texting don't always indicate chemistry.

25. Expect games.

26. Bring your expectations down to earth.

27. Remain upbeat in the face of inevitable rejection.

28. Break your dealbreakers.

29. Don't be the pen pal.

30. Send messages like a human.

31. Silence is a "no."

32. No. Dinner. Dates.

33 It's a date, not an interview.

A note on common sense.

Conclusion

Introduction

First things first – online dating has been around a **long time** in one form or another. It's not a new concept.

Remember that Tom Hanks and Meg Ryan classic, *You've Got Mail*? That movie was released in 1998. For reference, a little company that you might have heard of called *Google* was also founded in 1998...

If you'll recall, those were the days of clunky AOL chatrooms, chat sites, and forums.

What's changed in the world of online dating since?

- We've got fancier and sleeker looking apps and websites as opposed to those pixelated chatrooms. We're mobile now, and so are our online dating options.

- We've become curiously more driven by instant gratification, as apps like Tinder show. Yet we also desire curation and not having to wade through the masses, like the current crop of matchmaking companies shows.

- There are so many apps and sites that it's entirely possible to have a complete and even overwhelming dating life solely through online dating.

- Online dating is slowly and surely shedding any semblance of a stigma and simply becoming a smart way of meeting people outside of your normal circles.

And so on.

But sadly, in my experience as an online dating coach, **it would be a <u>big mistake</u> to say that we've similarly evolved in how *good* we are at online dating**.

As I'll analyze later, an online dating profile is an *odd combination between a resume and a pick-up line* that leaves people literally clueless as to how to present themselves. It throws people for a serious curve to have to represent themselves in a new medium… and it shows.

People don't know how to portray themselves in the best light, calibrate their online humor, choose their best pictures, message effectively, bridge the online/offline gap, and generally succeed in the online dating environment. And it applies to men and women equally.

I've decided that there is only so many times I can read that someone *"likes to go out but has no problem with a Netflix night staying in,"* or *"likes to travel and try new food."*

We can do better, people!

My name is **Patrick King** and I'm an online dating, dating, and social skills coach. Let me shepherd you through the whole process of online dating from an experienced perspective, and show you exactly how to build a spectacular profile, send alluring messages... and ultimately go on more dates to meet your match.

That's the ultimate goal, and these **33 commandments** I've gleaned from years of navigating the online dating minefield will take you through beginning to end of online dating – from getting over the psychological barriers and supposed stigma, to planning out the dates that you'll doubtlessly get after internalizing this book.

Some of my commandments might seem like common sense, but if it warrants my mentioning it, you better believe that it's the current sad state of affairs.

So let's get you out there and owning online dating.

1. You're online dating? Own it.

Listen, I know that you're going to have hang-ups about the fact that you are ***gasp*** online dating.

But guess what... **who cares**? Probably only you.

This is something for you to own and be proud of, because the people that will hate on it and make fun of you for doing it? Yeah, the ones that you'll be going on way more dates than, and who you are way more comfortable and secure than? They're just ashamed that they don't have the chutzpah to do it for themselves, and projecting that onto you.

That's the **real reason** that most people associate a stigma with online dating these days. It's the act of putting yourself out there so directly and aggressively.

It leaves room to be rejected, and many people aren't accustomed to that... and don't want to face it. Because when you put yourself out there to get rejected, it inevitably happens sometimes and leads to devaluing a self-esteem that some people really cannot afford.

But you? You're using online dating because you're smart, savvy, and above all else, pragmatic. Name me another way to meet quality single people that you can date tomorrow, all from the comfort of your own couch.

But in the meantime, **own the fact that you're online dating**. Leave your shame at the door, because there really shouldn't be any shame associated with it.

Not that you should eschew all actual human interaction in trying to meet your mate, but this enables you to cut down on time shouting interview questions to people in loud clubs and bars.

It was a common conversation I used to have.

"You're doing online dating?! Why?!"

"Um, have you seen the women I've been out with lately? Why wouldn't I?"

Enough said.

2. Online dating is the new organic.

Let's face it. You've stumbled down the rabbit hole, and there's no looking back.
Chances are that you know someone who has met their significant other from online dating. If you don't, your friends are lying to you.

And you know what? There's absolutely nothing wrong with it. Why should a stigma exist when all you're doing is **taking a proactive approach** to meeting new people? Recognizing that meeting new people trickles to a stop after school, and taking advantage of new technology available to us?

We can buy just about anything online these days. Why can't we search for a mate online too?

Welcome to the new organic.

Once you can embrace this fact, any mental barriers you have towards online dating should vanish in a second. All you're doing is using what is available to you, literally at your fingertips, and using it to spread your reach farther than you would be able to otherwise.

I think most of us inherently realize this, so what keeps the stigma of online dating well and alive? I would posit that it's **not really a stigma, and more of a defense mechanism** that people have.

In other words, people don't look down on online dating… they just wish they were more comfortable with the prospect of rejection like you. Once you put yourself out there willingly with the aim of finding someone. If you don't and fail, that's a rejection that people are not accustomed to thinking about. I covered this in the previous commandment.

But once we get past that, we know that it is **entirely too logical** to expand your potential dating pool beyond your immediate contacts and their friends.

Everyone wants to meet people organically, like a chance encounter at the grocery store, or reaching for the same pair of gloves in a shop and touching hands serendipitously.

But guess what? That doesn't happen. You don't live in a John Cusack rom-com, and even if it does happen, it's once in a blue moon. Why not speed up the process by enabling your own search on a daily basis?

So embrace the new organic way of meeting people – online.

3. Free sites are fine.

For some reason, and I honestly can't figure out the reason, people always say that paid sites are fair superior in quality of singles to free sites.

I suspect that this is because people assume that the presence of a paywall is enough of a barrier to entry to discourage "creeps" from using the site. Of course, there are a few reasons that this is an amazingly flawed assumption.

First, it assumes that no "creeps" have money. If anything, many "creeps" become so precisely *because* they have money.

Second, it assumes that "creeps" are deterred by having to pay for a dating site.

Third, it arbitrarily draws lines between your definition of desirable and undesirable, and assumes that the desireables (educated, higher salary, etc.) think the same way you do about the quality of singles on paid dating sites.

Most of all, it's just wrong.

Despite what people say about the relative qualities of people inhabiting paid and free sites, **do me a favor**. Skim through both sets of sites, OkCupid and Match, for example. Tell me how many faces you'll see in common. And then, tell me how much quicker you run out of options within any search parameters on the paid sites.

So not only are the userbases largely overlapping, there are far fewer people on paid sites for you to choose from.

So why would you exclusively use a paid site? I don't know, and can only tie it to people making assumptions that they provide absolutely zero information to back it up with. It's an amazingly losing proposition to exclusively use a paid site.

So here's my compromise – use both simultaneously. It's more work, but some things you just have to find out for yourself.

Finally, here's another perspective on the people that people that use paid dating sites. They're so desperate they have to pay for it? Now, of course I don't agree with it, but you're making the same judgments when you assume positive things about those who use paid dating sites.

Chew on that.

4. Seeing people you know is just like running into them at a bar.

One of the most common reasons that keep people away from online dating is the fact that they will inevitably run into someone they know on the site or app.

To which I reply: **So what? Are you going to explode from embarrassment? Why would they judge you if they're on it too?**

You see people you know everywhere in public, and you are probably happy if you see them at the mall or at a restaurant. You probably wave to them, say hello to catch up, and go about your own ways. This isn't the worst thing in the word, and can often brighten a day.

Let's take the most analogous in-person setting to an online dating site – a bar or club. This is the most analogous because you are dressed to impress, talking to the opposite sex, and generally presenting yourself in the favorable way that you are on an online dating site.

In other words, **you are trying to appear attractive both in your online dating profile, and at a club or bar**. Being honest, this is the root as to why we feel uncomfortable seeing people you know. You feel self-conscious with them knowing how you present yourself to the opposite sex in your most attractive light... because you think people might laugh at it.

But it is exactly the same as a bar or club setting, so why feel self-conscious about being on a dating site?

What happens when you see someone you know at a bar club? They don't care that you're trying to impress others – they're doing the same. You're in the same boat and have that mutual understanding. You have mutual or similar goals. It's completely normalized and not a big deal.

Now transfer that to online dating!

If you see someone you know on OkCupid, they've seen you too. Own it. You both are showing your A game, and that's nothing to be ashamed of. What's the problem?

5. Curate your online presence

Let's start by reviewing the medium that we're talking about in this book – online dating.

So since this operates in the **online space**... it's only logical that people will use the Internet and are somewhat Internet-proficient.

You will be Googled, lightly stalked, and semi-judged before you even meet based on the above.

Make sure that your first impression isn't ruined by that lewd limerick you wrote when you were 15, and **curate your online presence**!

This means to make sure to **deep Google yourself** – I'm talking page 10 results type deep – and figure out exactly what the internet has to say about you. Google your name + your job, your name + your home town, your name + your school(s), and so on.

Make sure all of your social media profiles have good pictures on them that aren't from when you originally set the profile up 4 years ago. Make sure the biographies and blurbs about yourself have good grammar, and accurately reflect what you're doing with your life in the present.

Make sure your Facebook profile is set to private, or at least the publicly available parts reflect well on you.

Finally, make sure that the username you use isn't identical to other places you've used it as an online handle... such as fetishkink.com/forums, or anything like that.

That's the common sense stuff... or so you'd think.

6. Online dating for women is not online dating for men.

If you've read any of my other online dating books or guides, you'll recall that I touch on the skewed economy of online dating. It echoes the real-life gender disparities, but to the tenth degree.

Dating in general is an area of life where men are at an amazing disadvantage. They are expected to be the pursuers, and are often competitive with each other.

This leads to the inevitable conclusion of men fighting over the same women… while many women are enabled to simply sit back, be courted, and take a passive role in their romantic lives. Of course, this is a vague generalization… but it's mostly true. Even if it doesn't apply to you personally, you have many female friends for which this holds painfully true.

And it's even truer with online dating.

Simply put, the online dating experience for men is drastically different from womens', so this should explain a few things.

Men: Why is my reply rate so low? Because of the gender ratio imbalance. She has too many messages to reply to.

Men: Why does she have nothing in her profile? Because of the gender ratio imbalance. She gets messages regardless of her profile completion.

Men: Why does she not even have the courtesy to reply to my message saying no thanks? Because of the gender ratio imbalance. She has too many messages to reply to.

Women: Why am I getting so many short, or copy and paste messages? Because of the gender ratio imbalance. Because guys don't get many replies in general, so they learn that it is a waste of time to craft thoughtful messages.

Women: Why do guys want to meet up so quickly? Because…. Well, you get it.

Every one of those questions can pretty much be answered with the gender economy of online dating.

Men are spread thin and aware that it's super competitive, so they often spend as little time as needed to try to move offline and otherwise interact with women.

Women are so overwhelmed with messages and potential dates that they don't have the time to reply to everyone – their issue is often curation.

So try to view your recipient/messaging partner/potential date/date through this lens. Everyone has it different, and how someone reacts to you is not necessarily a reflection of their opinion on you.

7. Don't rely only on online dating.

I touched upon this briefly earlier. When you engage in online dating, don't just rely on that as your sole method of meeting the opposite sex.

There are a few reasons to stay rooted in the real world and unplug every once in a while.

First, it can be extremely distracting.

Going out to a bar while messaging people on Tinder and OkCupid? Yup, been there. What's the point of even going out? Life was passing me by my very own eyes. It was a waste of time, as I couldn't do both competently and people are worse at multi-tasking than they realize.

Second, you miss a lot of chances to connect with people in real life if you're always buried in your apps and sites.

Meeting friends of friends is one of the most common ways to find a relationship, but you close yourself to such opportunities when you don't go out "because you are online dating." You may inadvertently cultivate a mindset that is very limiting.

Third, it's damn time consuming.

Don't let it consume you. If you dive in head first and commit to using each site to its fullest, it can be like a second full-time job.

Finally, you mindset towards the opposite sex will begin to get very skewed for lack of better term. You'll always be looking for the next best thing... because that's what you can do online.

Someone else, another date, is just a swipe or message away, and while I love that online dating has empowered people to fully grasp their sexuality, this mindset of abundance isn't conducive to forming long term attachments for many.

Just don't use online dating to fully replace real human interaction and you're golden.

8. Don't discount sites that are "only for hookups".

Let's take a little stroll through recent history and examine what the perceptions of online dating have been.

10 years ago: Um, it was cute in *You've Got Mail*, but anyone that does it in real life is a weirdo desperate loser. Now I'm going to go check my MySpace account and make sure my frosted tips are looking sweet.

5 years ago: Online dating? I don't know, I'd rather meet people organically… but maybe when that stops.

2 years ago: I have friends that got together and met their wives and husbands on OkCupid, Match, and eHarmony, so I guess I'm open to it…

Now: Yeah, so last night I went on a Tinder date, and next week I've got an Okcupid date. What's the newest app called? I gotta check that out!

Point being, perceptions change, and are often unfair and untrue. Sites that are "only for hookups" are rarely that way, and don't reflect the current status quo.

Take OkCupid.

People used to decry it as a site filled with people only looking for hookups. What's the sentiment these days? It's perfectly acceptable, and on par with Match, eHarmony, Zoosk, and all the other so-called "serious" dating sites. And of course, on the "serious" dating sites, it's not like people there don't look for hookups as well.

So Tinder, Hinge, Plenty Of Fish, and so on – why discount them for the same reason? Dating sites are only going to be used for hookups if they lack a critical mass of users, because with the critical mass of users comes a wide range of people looking for anything. So with Tinder, you may very well find people looking for long term relationships and not just looking to hook up.

People have their reasons for using anything.

If you discount dating sites and apps for reasons based on reputation or assumptions, you are cutting yourself seriously short.

9. Profiles actually matter.

We are damn shallow these days, as you can tell by Tinder, Hot or Not, and whatever the newest imitator to the throne is.

But that doesn't mean that pictures are the **only** thing that matter. If you started conversing with a hottie of the opposite sex, and they failed to use there/their/they're properly, couldn't spell their own name, and thought the earth was bigger than the sun... would you continue to talk to them?

Told you – not only looks matter!

Here's how it works with most online dating.

The picture is the **first filter**. The picture is the gatekeeper through which you must pass to have a shot at the goal. But if you make it pass that first filter, you have to pass the **second filter** of the personality and profile test!

On sites where you have a profile, this is especially important (obviously). With apps like Tinder, it is less important, but your initial messages – the content, grammar, and level of interesting substance – *they serve as your profile*.

So while I will implore you to invest in some good pictures to make it through the gatekeeper, realize that you can't skate by on just great pictures alone.

The people that you'll meet that way won't really be interested in anything lasting, or you at all, because you haven't connected with them at all. You're operating on a shallow level of interaction that is fine for some nights, but mostly boring and unfulfilling.

10. Scope out your competition.

One of the themes in my writing and coaching is to be the best version of yourself. This means that you shouldn't be trying to imitate others, and use your own strengths to forge your identity.

This should obviously happen online in the way that you represent yourself and talk about your interests and hobbies.

But there is a ton of value in thinking about what other people are writing – checking out your competition – to see how you can differentiate yourself. After all, if you're presenting yourself in the same fashion as other people, despite it being your true interests and hobbies, then improvement is possible and in order. Superficially, most of us are pretty homogenous, so it's important to realize that and learn how to stand out.

Cough – traveling, eating, using the word "transplant", and saying that you're the type of person that can go out or hang out at home with a movie.

So what exactly do you gain when you scope out you competition?

You find out what's generic and overused in terms of ways to answer profile questions, terms, keywords, hobbies, and phrases. You like trying new food? Congratulations, welcome to the human race. Think of a more unique and interesting way to present it, like describing your weekly Iron Chef roommate contests.

You find out what other men/women are doing to differentiate themselves. Feel free to steal some great phrases you'll inevitably find in other people's profiles!

You can see examples of good profiles to see exactly what you're up again, and determine how much more effort your profile and online dating presence requires.

Yes, you should remain the best version of yourself. Don't imitate others or hide aspects of your personality. But that doesn't necessarily mean you can't present it in different and unique ways!

After all, online dating as you should be frustratingly familiar with by now, is all about presentation, quick hits, and first glances.

11. Don't answer profile questions literally.

Most of my clientele tends to want help with OkCupid profiles.

Other sites have profile questions pretty much the same question just re-phrased, but let's use **OkCupid profile questions** as a reference here.

Here are some of their questions that will be particularly good examples for this commandment:

- 6 things I could never do without;
- I spend a lot of time thinking about;
- On a typical Friday night I am.

One of the biggest mistakes I see, with clients or otherwise, is that they answer these questions way too literally.

Typically, they can't live without air, food, water, phone, laughter, friends, family, good times, coffee, etc. I mean, come on.

Do you really think this is what people want to know about you? That you're a human?

Just the knowledge alone that most people answer this question like this should deter people from doing it, but it sure doesn't.

<u>What this question is really asking is</u>: what are 6 things that are personal and unique to you that you really like? Yes, it's a harder question to answer, but that's the price if you want to win at online dating.

Next, I spend a lot of time thinking about... food, work, your next meal, your next vacation trip, etc.

Again, I know that more than 60% of the profiles I read are going to contain at least some of these elements. <u>This question is really asking</u> for you to showcase your creativity and list some of your greatest "what if" or "would you rather" questions. Creativity, if you haven't noticed, is the name of the game.

Finally, what are you doing on a typical Friday night? Just chilling after work, maybe grabbing a drink, then relaxing at home with my dog. Or alternatively, either going out with friends or chilling at home with Netflix.

<u>That question is really asking</u>: what does a fun night with you look like? What are fun, creative, and unique night-time activities that you have engaged in, or want to? To answer this literally will make you sound incredibly boring.

I hope I've induced some cringes above.

So try to get to the bottom of each profile question and deduce what a better, and more creative angle is to answer with.

12. Don't talk about things that can be easily disproved.

I guess I mostly mean brag.

Don't *brag* about things that can be easily disproved through your profile, your pictures, within the first page of Google search results, or by meeting.

But also don't *talk* about them.

I mean things like saying you're a snappy dresser, your height, your job description and history, how much you work out, and so on. The theme there, as I feel compelled to repeat again, is that they can easily be disproved or disagreed with.

You say you're a snappy dresser? Well, that's subjective, and someone could look at your pictures, decide the opposite, and label you as lacking self-awareness.

You say you're 6 foot when you're really 5 foot 9? Well, what if she decides to wear heels and dwarfs you at the bar?

You say you're a manager/director? Wait your company website or LinkedIn says you're just an analyst who was hired 2 months ago.

You say you work out a ton? Wait, your pictures show some serious muffin topping and chins. Well then.

As you can see, it only works against you if you can't back up what you say, at least in a superficial way that will hold up to minimal scrutiny. Once people find you out to be false, there are a bunch of other assumptions of dishonesty they will make about you, and it's just a bad party from there on.

Don't brag about things that are largely subjective, or that can be disproved easily.

13. But do editorialize in your profile.

I should first address the difference between bragging about something that can be disproved, IE lying, and editorializing in your profile.

Truth: You sometimes volunteer with autistic kids. Sometimes = once every couple of months when you don't have flag football or shopping obligations.

Lying: I run a program that works with autistic kids on the weekends.

Editorializing: I like to work with developmentally disabled children on weekends as often as I can, I find the impact I can make incredibly gratifying.

See the difference?

Editorializing your profile is spinning things to make yourself sound great, but staying with the *sphere of truth*. This is exactly what you should do with your profile, because remember – it's a weird mixture between a resume and a pick-up line.

So while you want to come off humble and not overly braggy, remember that your overall goal is still to sell yourself to whoever you feel your target customer is. And the way you sell yourself to a potential employer? *"Yeah, I can handle that." "Yeah, I ran that initiative." "I'm experienced in that application and really enjoy it!"*

Online dating profiles are no different. You just want to come off as best as possible, and give off the strongest first impression that you possibly can. Remember that just as certain jobs are suited to certain people, you shouldn't try to appeal to everyone. But for those within your target fit, you should make yourself sound as interesting as possible.

Here's another quick example: You went to Spain for 2 weeks last year and don't really remember much of it.

How about… you lived life through the pages of your sketchbook as you ate, drank, and hosteled your way through Spain's castles and underground art scene? You get it.

14. Invest in your pictures.

I know that I've said that pictures aren't everything, and that profiles actually matter... but pictures are the **first gatekeeper and line of defense** you have to your goal, whatever it may be.

It's the first impression that you make on people, and really determines the rest of the tone of the interaction, or if there even is one.

So it's silly to not strive to use the best pictures of ourselves as possible.

Why then, do we just pull pictures from Facebook or other social media sites? It's too often that I see people put in minimal effort with their pictures – 5 minutes scanning Facebook to end up with a picture that is probably a little grainy, low-definition, cropped with a phantom arm around your neck, and 2 years old.

That, a great first impression does not make.

When I say to invest in your pictures, I mean to really make an effort. I know that for many, putting in the minimal amount of effort into online dating is the only way you'll do it... because putting in any more effort and subsequently failing is not a good feeling.

But hey, if you're going to do something, you might as well try to do it right and optimally. If you want to win at online dating, you will put some effort into your pictures.

It doesn't have to be over the top, like doing a professional photo shoot. I actually recommend against that because those pictures will be overly processed and posed. You want your profile pictures to still look natural and in the flow of daily life, not like a professional headshot as if you were auditioning for an off-broadway play.

Here's my optimal level of investment I recommend for you: pick out two outfits that you look great in and feel great in. Head a park with a friend that has a DSLR, or otherwise decent camera. Have them take a bunch of candid pictures of you walking around, interacting with nature, and generally smiling. Don't do poses.

Buy beer and pizza for your friend, and have fun sorting through all the pictures.

15. Brag with caution.

Online dating is only one thing at its core – a marketplace that is driven through sales. This means that you need to be able to sell yourself – brag about yourself – in a tasteful and effective way.

How do you do this? It's tough because an online dating profile is some weird bastard mixture between a resume and a pick-up line.

<u>First, two universal truths.</u>

1 – No one likes a braggart.

2 – No one likes too much modesty or low self-esteem.

How do you find a balance?

Here is a set of guidelines for you to follow when positioning yourself as the ripest avocado in the store:

First, don't outright brag about your abilities or skills. People usually brag in a funny, backhanded, or self-deprecating way.

Second, bragging about sweet, cute, funny, unique, stupid, or OBJECTIVELY awesome things is acceptable. This is because it is not typically directly about you, instead about an emotion that was evoked.

Third, anything that serves to directly talk about how high-value you are should be disguised with humor or self-deprecation.

Fourth, if you brag outright, you better have a legitimate claim and be prepared to be judged on it.

Fifth, as I've mentioned before, don't brag about things that people can contradict in your profile immediately. If you write that you are a grammar nazi, you better not have any grammatical errors.

Sixth, embrace the false modesty of the subtle humblebrag – a statement that is a putdown of yourself, but simultaneously a brag.

Seventh, when people brag, they usually use congruent body language and tone of voice. You can't do this online.

Eighth, it's typically more acceptable to brag about something that's happened to you, versus something you've accomplished.

Ninth, is this something you actually want to brag about, and that will be attractive to the opposite sex?

Above all else, can you say your brag out loud with a straight face?

Bragging online is a thin line, and can instantly send up a red flag if done incorrectly. Take caution!

16. Perform constant eye-roll checks.

There's something about the inherent unfamiliarity with online dating that most people have that makes them say **amazingly weird things** about themselves.

I've likened it to a **weird marriage between a resume and a pick-up line**. Flipping through profiles on a daily basis, it's clear to me that most people don't really know how to navigate that or what tone to use.

Sometimes it's funny, while other times it is absolutely **cringe-worthy**.

But it's surprisingly easy to avoid saying things that are uncharacteristic, overly vague, or just plain weird.

Perform constant eye-roll checks, and have your friends do it for you as well. Read over your profile, and make sure that there are no sentences where they just look at you and say "Really?"

This serves to help you in two ways.

First, it keeps you on the straight and narrow. It safeguards you from saying things that you normally wouldn't in real life. It ensures that you aren't committing any foul errors, and that your profile won't cause people to wonder what you were smoking when you wrote it. If you scoff at this point, you haven't been online dating long enough.

Second, it keeps you true to your identity, and helps you bring out the "you" in your profile as opposed to what you think you're supposed to sound like. Performing the eye-roll check, especially with friends, makes sure that you're representing who you truly are, instead of a generic list of adjectives.

Keep in mind that your overall goal in your profile is to sell yourself by distinguishing yourself from the rest of your competition. Eye-roll checks make sure that your 'offering' is objectively attractive, and capitalizes on your unique traits.

17. Spellchck your profile and messages.

Grammar too.

18. Humor usually needs congruent body language.

Who's your favorite comedian?

Now how do they **look** when they deliver a joke? How do they **sound**?

Most importantly, how would their delivery be if you were forced to **read** their joke **without** seeing them? Would the joke have the same impact, or would it be confusing and possibly offensive?

There are many different types of humor, but nearly all of them require **congruent body language**, facial expressions, and tone of voice to be pulled off to any degree.

Just think about the last joke you made. You probably said it with a wry smile, a cock of your head, or used a gesture to bring it home. If you ever say things with a shit-eating grin that indicates that you mean the opposite of what you've just said, then you better be doubly careful.

Even with dead-pan humor, the tone of voice and the humorously-serious facial expression is what indicates to people that you're joking.

Guess what online dating doesn't allow you to have? Smileys, "hahas," and other online indicators of emotion aren't always sufficient to indicate that you're joking or trying to make a joke. It can turn a statement like "Great parking job." into something sarcastic or hostile.

This commandment isn't so much of an instructive one, rather an awareness one. If you're aware that much of your humor can and will be misconstrued, it will force you to think about the way you present yourself in your profile and messages.

You may also have to find another way to demonstrate your sense of humor online if you find that you are overly sarcastic in nature. It would be helpful to analyze your text interaction with your friends to see just what kind of humor you typically use, and if they ever misconstrue what you say despite knowing you and your sense of humor well.

Now if your friends misconstrue what you say, think about how much more likely it is that a stranger would!

As a perpetual jokester, I often have to think about what kind of humor the other person enjoys and would even recognize.

19. Stories are king; adjective lists are not.

Being an online dating coach, you might imagine that I've seen a few online dating profiles in my time.

One of the most frustrating things to read in a profile is the dreaded adjective list. You know what I'm referring to.

I'm laidback, happy, funny, like to laugh, and super adventurous!

Okay... honestly, who did you NOT just describe? The list of adjectives is so general that it actually **says nothing at all**. It's like describing a human that likes to drink water, eat food, sleep, empty their bowels, and interact with others.

Even specific adjectives are practically worthless in online dating profiles because they just don't really say anything about the person. You can present yourself in whatever manner you want with your adjectives, but it's ultimately all **white noise** and a sentence that people skim over because it makes no impact.

Adjectives are useless. (I know I've said that already, but I just felt the need to emphasize it again.)

So if adjective lists aren't the way to describe yourself in an online dating profile, what's a better alternative?

Stories are king.

Don't fall into the trap of trying to describe your entire being within the space of a short paragraph blurb. That's impossible, and you'll do yourself a disservice because you will inevitably just use general and superficial terms.

Instead, all you want to do in your profile is showcase aspects of your personality through short stories. When you say that you're adventurous, it falls on deaf ears because it's something that most people would describe themselves as.

But when you tell a short story about how you went to a yak rodeo in the Himalayas, that gives a bit clearer or a picture of how adventurous you actually are, and separates you from the pack of other online dating denizens.

Funny? Tell a story about how you played a prank on someone.

Laidback? Tell a story about how you stayed calm within the fray of the Running with the Bulls in Pamplona.

20. You won't appeal to everyone.

I talk about this in my other books as calibration – by presenting the best version of yourself in a true and accurate manner, you will project your actual identity and appeal to those who it resonates with.

This is not going to be everyone.

Likewise, not everyone appeals to you. When you think about it like that, it becomes a very obvious fact of human nature. We like what we like, and even superficially, we know when someone just isn't our type.

However, the way most people represent themselves online is completely contrary to this notion. People usually try to appeal to everyone and appear as neutral as possible on a wide range of topics. This is so they can cast as wide a net as possible, and not offend anyone. They become a sanitized and frankly boring version of themselves to reach that goal.

We sell ourselves seriously short when we do this.

The simple truth is that you won't appeal to everyone in online dating. Fair or not, you're not everyone's type. So realizing this, it's a much, **much** smarter proposition instead to emphasize unique attributes about yourself to attract those who ARE your type. Those who will identify with you on a deep and personal level, and those who will like the unsanitized, real version of yourself.

It just saves everyone's time.

Here's a short example to show just what I mean.

I'm not religious. For a while I avoided answering all types of match questions about religion, and listed my religion as something to the effect of "spiritual, but not religious" or something similarly vague. I didn't want to offend any potential date that happened to be religious.

But... that's a little silly, isn't it? Because me and a religious girl would likely have very different values and priorities, and I would just be wasting my time to try to date one. So why was I trying to appeal to them?

It would have been a waste of both of our time and I fared much better just being myself and trying to appeal to those similar to me.

So if you present as the best version of your true self, you won't appeal to everyone... but you'll appeal to those who appeal to you!

21. Re-think what you want in a partner.

If we're 100% honest with ourselves, we have a pretty extensive list of things that we want in our partners. Hopefully we don't take the view that they are hard requirements as such, and just preferences… but the line gets extremely blurred from time to time.

Education, job, salary, background, language, ethnicity, hometown, hobbies, interests – these are all things that we might think about when we visualize our future partner. I'm not saying that it's wrong to have that visualization, but it can create unrealistic expectations and entitlements. And by no coincidence I'm sure, with online dating you can filter for almost every one of those factors.

So when you're online dating, you have the ability to focus on things that you might think that matter. You'll be faced with a veritable buffet on a daily basis because you can filter for exactly those things that you think you want, and ignore literally everyone else. Of course, this has its positives and negatives.

The biggest negatives are twofold.

First, you miss out on people that don't fall within the arbitrary filters that you've selected. Maybe someone is an inch shorter or taller than what you're searching for, or perhaps someone doesn't have the keyword "soccer" in their profile. This makes it literally a dealbreaker for you because you won't even have the opportunity to meet or see them... and this is all as a result of focusing on some very superficial traits (of course, we do it regardless).

Second, you seriously end up focusing on the wrong things. A relationship is going to be a multiple year decision – say 60 years? So if you're focusing on that one inch of height, that alma mater, or that interest of soccer... well those things aren't going to matter in the next year, likely. So why depend on them to take you through the next 59 years?

What matters in a healthy, growing long-term relationship is your **personal day-to-day chemistry, respect for each other, and being challenged by each other**. The other stuff is for the most part just nice to have, but it's a difficult thing to embrace with online dating.

22. Don't be paranoid, but be smart.

Every couple of years, online dating makes a negative splash in the national media because someone drugged, raped, and killed their date. Fingers get pointed, and it's unclear as to who is really at fault with the entire situation.

Of course, this drastically ignores the fact that each and every week, someone is assaulted or molested on a normal date that didn't come from online dating. Online dating is still subject to being sensationalized in the media, and it conveniently overlooks more frightening statistics about normal dating and date rape.

The point I'm making is that while online dating carries some inherent dangers with it, I wouldn't call it more dangerous than meeting someone via normal dating, which people almost never bat an eye at.

This is all a judgment and assumption assigned to online dating when it was (1) in its infancy and did truly contain some unhinged and dangerous people, and (2) association with Craigslist casual encounters, hookers, and the like. That is not the vast majority of online dating these days.

But of course, you should still be safe whenever you're meeting someone that you don't already know, even if they are vouched for by a friend or through your network.

Let your friends/roommate/family know that you'll be on a date, and to check in with you every few hours just to make sure that you are responsive and in good shape.

If it sounds fishy, it probably is fishy. Don't meet someone in an abandoned warehouse unless you want to wake up in a tub of ice missing a kidney.

Don't give out personally identifiably info until you have to, and especially not your home address and things of that nature. Don't have people drop you off at home, instead opt for up a block or two.

Pepper spray? I support it.

Even if it seems unnecessary, it is literally almost zero effort to take safeguards and ensure your safety. After all, many a famous last words have been "It will be fine..."

23. Don't assume exclusivity.

Now this is something I've found to be amazingly online dating-centric, and sort of a new phenomenon. A few years ago before online dating took the world by storm, people dated largely whoever was in their social circle, and whoever was **tangential** to it.

Naturally, this limited the potential dating pool considerably, and the consequences were that people often only dated one person at a time. Now, this is something I support because it allows you to actually focus your efforts onto one person and take the time to invest in them and make an effort to see if there is a real connection and not just lust.

But online dating has literally opened the world up for your potential dating pool. No longer is it constrained to those that you see around your office and friends of friends… and this means that with the opportunity, people will certainly seek to explore those options. Much of the time, simultaneously.

A new person to date is just a swipe or message away, and when the barriers to entry are that low, you can bet that you yourself will take advantage of it too!

So ask yourself this: are you only pursuing one person at a time these days? Are you shutting off all other advances if you've gone on 3 dates with someone? How about even if you're having sex with someone?

I'm betting the answer is a big fat "No."

To be clear, there's absolutely nothing wrong with this. I'm about as sex positive of a person as you'll meet, and judging people based on wanting to date multiple people at once? Get out of here.

I just want to make the point that any assumptions you have about someone that you feel that you've really bonded with – it's still wise to have that exclusivity and "what are we?" talk at some point, and you can't just assume that they aren't seeing anyone else.

You also might want to think about not putting all of your eggs in one basket, so to speak. This doesn't mean you shouldn't give people your undivided attention and the respect they deserve, however.

24. Messaging and texting don't always indicate chemistry.

We all have that one friend who is simply terrible at communication. They'll take hours to reply to a simple text, not mention that they will be late until 5 minutes after they were supposed to arrive, and generally just be difficult to interpret.

And despite all that, whenever you get together, you head home with your sides aching from laughter.

It becomes clear that they don't mean to neglect you or make you feel like you're not a priority – they're just legitimately bad at communicating and replying to people in a timely manner. This doesn't make them any worse of a person, nor does it reflect how they feel about you.

Any of this starting to sound familiar? Keeping in mind what we know about the difference in online dating experiences for men and women, could there be other factors at play when you're messaging or texting with someone?

So the back and forth banter that you want to imagine there being with your new mate – it might not exist, and that's completely okay. Try to refrain from making judgments based on the frequency of their texting and initiating contact, and just realize that some people aren't great at it.

Consequently, the chemistry that you will experience in-person with them might not accurately represent how the communications have been.

And of course, the lack of communications might be intentional as an introduction to the dating games that most people tend to play... in which case, I've got another commandment you should read!

25. Expect games.

Dating games are something that everyone claims to hate partaking in.

They are usually described as manipulative, dishonest, unnecessary, and generally beneath people.

Yet we instinctually don't shower people with attention, make our true intentions known, or text people back immediately. We filter what we say about our feelings towards them, and don't let our inner monologues see the light of day. We manipulate our availability and appear disinterested even when we're not.

It's because we (most of us, anyway) understand what drives basic human psychology, and what drives it definitely isn't what's easy and available. We strive for what's unattainable, a challenge, intriguing, and mysterious, because that achievement is so much more fulfilling.

When something is easily within our grasp, instead of basking in the triumph, we instantly think "*Wait, is this even worth it if it's so easy? Could I do better?"* and we don't want it anymore.

Finally let's be honest... despite how hard we try and how many attractive traits she might possess otherwise, it's hard to not be repulsed when she starts blowing up our phone and asking to hang out every night.

So how much game playing is really optimal in dating... and should the answer be zero?

It's a tough question to answer... but as I've told my clients, you can choose to date one of two ways: successfully by playing the requisite amount of games, or unsuccessfully by being completely yourself.

We recognize that challenge and intrigue drives attraction for others, and this can't help but inform our decisions on how to act while dating.

When phrased as thus, we can frame it much more positively as just being intelligent with how much to divulge about yourself as opposed to acting manipulative. *Don't blow up her phone. Don't always be the one to initiate conversations. Don't contact her three times in a row.*

Where's the game playing in that?

26. Bring your expectations down to earth.

I've already briefly covered the expectations and requirements that online dating can enable people to heap onto their perspective mates.

This is because of the filters that online dating utilizes, and because the next date is just a swipe or message away.

But just because it's natural to have built up expectations about your mate doesn't mean that it is correct or healthy.

This commandment is about keeping your expectations in line with reality, and oftentimes... dialing them down.

If you expect your date to have gone to X school, make Y annually in salary, and be more fit than Adonis himself... **are you yourself on that level and deserving of that**?

Would someone of that high caliber that you would demand actually be attracted to you and all of your accomplishments, traits, interests, and flaws? Are you being realistic, amazingly optimistic, *or do you live in a fantasy-land*?

There's another message within bringing your expectations down and all the associated real talk. Take the time to work on yourself, because you should be striving towards the best version of yourself. If you want someone that makes Y annually, or has Z interest, what are you doing to make that a reality for yourself? **Everyone wants a catch, but not everyone is willing to put in the effort to become a catch themselves**!

Another note on expectations specifically regarding a first date from someone you've met via online dating. Bring them down to zero and that will be just about the right level. There's just so much unpredictability about how someone's persona transfers from their profile, to texting/messaging, to real life.

And of course, pictures aren't always untouched and current… **Catfishing is very real, people**.

27. Remain upbeat in the face of inevitable rejection.

I'm going to be very honest here. Rejection is inevitable with online dating.

But here's the great part – it almost always has nothing to do with you personally. So it's something that shouldn't bother you... though that is much easier simply said than done.

Through a variety of factors that I won't get into in this commandment, online dating is reduced to a ridiculous numbers game at some point. That is, for every 10 messages you send out, you might only get replies from anywhere from 1-6 of them... therefore, it's important to keep your expectations in line with reality.

Rejection and failure are simply inevitable! But if they're not judging and rejecting you, then what are they judging and rejecting?

Here's a partial list; notice that YOU aren't on it.

1. The way you wrote your profile.
2. Your ability to play the online game.
3. A sliver of your personality that didn't pique their curiosity.
4. Completely shallow and superficial factors, or alternatively falling out of their arbitrary filters (like being 1 inch too short).

5. Reasons 100% unrelated to you, such as them becoming serious with someone else.
6. Literally nothing. Accounts are deactivated and abandoned every day, or they won't see your message through the sheer weight of their other conversations and messages. So they won't even take the time to read your message.

Feel better? Maybe not. But the point is that even though rejection will happen and still sting from time to time, developing your ability to casually brush it off, not take things so personally, and grow thicker skinned is key to owning online dating.

It's also important to learn to not take rejection in online dating personally, because that will just hamstring your ability to put yourself out there in a medium that demands that people take action.

28. Break your dealbreakers.

I mentioned earlier that you should re-think what you want in a partner, and attempt to resist using the arbitrary filters as closely as you might be tempted to otherwise.

Now let's think about things from the **opposite perspective**.

Instead of the traits that you are seeking and view as requirements, what about the traits that you think you are simply incompatible with and avoid like the plague? Otherwise known as **dealbreakers**.

What dealbreakers do you think you possess? This is a discussion that ranges far beyond the context of online dating, but is still very relevant within it because of the ways that you can filter your searches and be ridiculously choosy with the people that you talk to.

Whatever dealbreakers you think you have – *stop it now*.

Learn to recognize the difference between real, actual, destructive dealbreakers, and mere preferences... and I say this because it's all too common to hear a laundry list of things that people **think** that they need, or can't live without.

Height, school, salary, hometown, ethnicity, etc. You're entitled to your preferences of course, but should any of those (or their lack thereof) really determine whether you stay with someone or not?

I'm going to venture... no.

Here's an easy way to tell if your purported dealbreaker truly is one. Imagine that you start dating a great person. Everything is just electric and you get along swimmingly. They get your sense of humor. Sex is off the charts. The good stuff.

Then you find out that they don't make as much as you thought, or perhaps they smoke... or perhaps are mostly vegan.

If this going to be a big deal to you at that point, when you've already established great chemistry with them and like them otherwise? In other words, **if something doesn't tear you apart after you start dating them, it's not a dealbreaker.**

The big things that might matter once you're in that position are whether or not they want kids, religion, values and morality... those are most of the real dealbreakers that exist for most people.

Try to break your mindset of dealbreakers!

29. Don't be the pen pal.

Don't be the person who is content is message back and forth for eons before even thinking about wanting to meet up or go on a date.

And...

Don't be the person who is so petrified of rejection and the tenuous hold they have on the person that they are messaging that they push off asking for a date for weeks until the other person likely is bored already.

Either of those resonate with anyone?

This commandment definitely pertains more to men than women, but women are certainly guilty of this. The reason I say it pertains more to men is because with online dating, as with offline dating, they are typically the aggressors and take charge of the interaction.

People, you're on a dating site/app. The sole purpose is to meet with someone in person and determine if you like each other enough to keep seeing each other or not. It's a pretty simple concept. *You're not going to shock anyone if you ask them out*!

With more 'traditional' online dating options such as Match and OkCupid, the ideal message to ask someone out is after 3-6 exchanges. If you've made it there, congratulations! The date is essentially yours to lose, and that's as good of a green light as you're going to get from her. Ask her out.

With dating apps, it's a bit different because it's more of a free-flowing, constant conversation that might necessitate more messages before rapport is built.

If you keep waiting, she'll be waiting too... and likely get tired of waiting. As we all know about the economics of online dating, females are in much higher demand, and there's a good chance she will be scooped up by any of the other 2-5 guys she is talking to simultaneously.

So there are 2 clear components to not being a pen pal, in my mind.

First, you're wasting people's time if you don't have the intention of meeting up in the near future.

Second, you're painting yourself in a negative light, because many women will expect guys to take the lead, and will not look favorably upon those that do not.

Asking someone out is easy if you know that they'll say yes – but they'll never tell you YES. Luckily, the length of an interaction is a pretty good indicator to their green light signals.

30. Send messages like a human.

Just as people oftentimes let the unfamiliarity of the online dating environment influence them to write downright weird things in their profile, they'll write downright weird things in their messages as well.

Actually, it can range from weird, creepy, offbeat, to confusing and nonsensical.

But all of that can be solved with the following mindset: **all you're doing is starting a conversation with someone.** *How would you do this in person?*

Here's a short list of things you **shouldn't** do:

- Cut and paste the same thing to everyone.
- Put them on a pedestal.
- Too many compliments.
- Grammatical and punctuation mistakes.
- Be overly sexual and aggressive.
- Ask 10 questions in a row, up front.
- Badger them with messages if there is no reply.

Now to things that you SHOULD do?

Well how would you start a conversation in real life? Besides simply saying "Hi," maybe you'd lean in and make a joke about the crazy woman in line, or remark that their shirt reminded you of a tropical bird. Any of these openers are 1-3 sentences… because that's the way you start an actual conversation naturally. They are indirect, not aggressive, and give them something to reply to.

So why do so many people write paragraphs upon paragraphs about themselves, the woman, and an analysis of every little thing their profiles have in common? It's not uncommon to see messages complete with an introduction, thesis, and conclusion.

What if you did this in person? *"Hey, I also like to rock climb and watch Game of Thrones. Oh, also, did you know that Game of Thrones was filmed in [location]? I see you also went to Thailand, I did too 3 years ago! How are you liking Boston? My sister is a nurse too, and she loves her job."*

My head is spinning just from writing that.

Keep this in mind: your initial message is just to start a conversation as organically as the medium allows and simply **GET A REPLY** – not seduce them or enthrall them. Hopefully that takes the pressure off that first message for you.

31. Silence is a "no thank you."

This is perhaps one of the most annoying aspects of being able to rely on texting and messaging as the main means of communication.

Silence, or the lack of a reply, almost always indicates "Thanks, but no thanks".
I could go on a whole rant about why this has contributed to the degradation of our social skills, people skills, communication skills, ability to confront people… and how it's generally helped us become more distant and unsympathetic to people…

But I won't.

Instead, I'll just say the following: along with the new organic of online dating, there is a new level of courteousness where silence is perfectly acceptable as a "no thanks," and indeed sometimes is preferable to affirmatively saying no or acknowledging someone.

This will happen at each stage of your online interaction… and even after you meet in person.

If you message someone and they don't reply to you, it's not because they didn't see your message or were hit by a car on their way back to their computer. That obviously happens from time to time (not seeing your message), but my point is that **the lack of a response shouldn't really be something for you to try to interpret**.

If after a date, they don't reply to your inquiring about the next time they're free, they didn't fall off a cliff during their last bike ride. They just aren't feeling it, and silence is a much easier way to express that than to have to send the "I'm sorry, I'm just not feeling it" text.

If there's one message you can take from this commandment, it's that **silence is a hint**. Not a particularly strong one, but a *widely accepted one* that usually leads to "no".

This entire commandment is basically an introduction to the new texting and communication rules and how to take a hint these days.

32. No. Dinner. Dates.

I could go on a whole rant about this, but dinner dates aren't organic, don't allow for flirting, separate you physically, lock you in for a set amount of time, force you to stare at each other, and create pressure to have constant conversation and banter.

Instead, make an activity the star of the date.

It's a far more organic and natural way of conversing when you don't have to make constant noise, and everything that the dinner date doesn't allow, an activity does: flirtation, touching, physical closeness, fluid time constraints, and the ability to pick your conversation spots.

You can even just take a walk! As it happens, all of a woman's sexual characteristics are on full display and showcased when she walks... so she will feel good about it, and so will you. Walking is amazingly underrated. It allows you to flirt, touch, tease, bump, and otherwise interact in ways that you can't when you're stationary.

And during your walk... walk to a few different spots from your initial meeting venue.

This has both a practical and chemistry component.

It's practical because having a part of a date end after an hour allows you to evaluate whether you want to continue the date or even see them again. It will also allow you to gauge their interest by seeing their reaction to your suggestion of extending the date once or twice.

Chemistry-wise, planning your date in segments is extremely powerful.

Say you're meeting your date at the dog park. You could part ways after an hour, or continue to the nearby ice cream parlor. Then continue on to dinner. Then continue to a cool bar that serves your favorite gimlet.

You know how people use the term getting swept off their feet? This is exactly what that does. It creates a veritable whirlwind feeling because you've essentially had four mini-dates in one night. This fosters comfort and familiarity.

And fellas: you also get the chance to take control of the interaction and date by laying out the options and making the final decision on where you are going and how you are going to get there. I can't count how many times I have been told that women love a man who can take charge and not be passive.

33 It's a date, not an interview.

There's nothing more disappointing than showing up to a date all pumped up, only for the conversation to fall flat on its face and chemistry to slither down a nearby drain. The whole thing is just devoid of any spark, and carries on like an interview.

What characterizes an interview, as opposed to a conversation, flirtatious or not?

Exchanging "*How about you's*", jumping from topic to topic, and dry and shallow subject matter.

It's great that you went to college a few miles away from each other, but can we go a little bit deeper than that? It's true that a big part of chemistry is feeling each other out and finding commonalities to connect on, but the shallow stuff doesn't really do the job.

It's the deep commonalities – the whys and hows – that really bond people together, not a mutual friend named Jorge.

The problem is that we can't just ask for deep commonalities, as many people will feel violated by questions like that. People also don't really volunteer them until they come up organically in conversation, if at all.

The easy solution to this is **treat your life like a series of stories**. Think about all of the mundane date questions that you'll be asked and prepare an engaging, short story about it. This allows conversation to flow smoothly and go in directions that you never would have otherwise.

How was your weekend? *Fun! How about yours?*

Meh. How about this:

How was your weekend? *Amazing, I took a drive down to Tallahassee and saw a car made entirely of shag carpet!*

Or even better:

How was your weekend? *Not too shabby, I went rock climbing outside for the first time and got over my fear of heights!*

See how that answer is even better by including things that are personal to you, that other people can relate to easily? Your date will be compelled to ask about rock climbing or your fear of heights.

Treat your date like a *date* – your goal is to connect with someone, and that the way to do that is through personal stories that convey who you are and what you like to do. Leave the interview for later.

A note on common sense.

You'd be surprised.

Conclusion

Hopefully what you've gained from this book is that the entire concept of online dating seriously throws people for a loop, and a ton of common sense simply flies out the door.

You yourself might be guilty of it, but after reading this book and harnessing its lessons, you'll be readily armed and prepared to own online dating. I believe that I've given you a great overview of the entire online dating process – from the correct approaches and mindsets, to nitty gritty technical and procedural questions.

I'm a results-oriented type of person, and that's what I try to impart in my books – actionable steps and items for you to work on. It's not a full-length novel, but I would expect that you seriously re-evaluated your profile and messaging throughout reading this, or took some notes. That would be the optimal way to read and re-read this book.

I want to help you succeed with online dating, and have imparted years of my coaching experience distilled into 33 digestible nuggets.

Above all else, I hoped to crack the stigma behind online dating and make clear the real reasons people sometimes decry it. Embrace it and own it.

I wish you the best with your online dating endeavors!

Sincerely,

Patrick King
Dating and Social Skills Coach
www.PatrickKingConsulting.com

P.S. If you enjoyed this book, please don't be shy and drop me a line, leave a review, or both! I love reading feedback, and reviews are the lifeblood of Kindle books, so they are always welcome and greatly appreciated.

Other books by Patrick King include:

Did She Reply Yet? The Gentleman's Guide to Owning Online Dating (OkCupid & Match Edition) http://www.amazon.com/dp/B00HESY42G

Charm Her Socks Off: Creating Chemistry from Thin Air http://www.amazon.com/dp/B00IEO688W

MAGNETIC: How to Impress, Connect, and Influence http://www.amazon.com/dp/B00ON8WJKY